Home at Last

Home at Last

Poems by

Steven Kent

© 2025 Steven Kent. All rights reserved.
This material may not be reproduced in any form, published,
reprinted, recorded, performed, broadcast,
rewritten, or redistributed without
the explicit permission of Steven Kent.
All such actions are strictly prohibited by law.

Cover design by Shay Culligan
Cover image by Steven Kent

ISBN: 978-1-63980-744-4
Library of Congress Control Number: 2025937856

Kelsay Books
502 South 1040 East, A-119
American Fork, Utah 84003
Kelsaybooks.com

Thank you to Sandy Helgeson, my wonderful, supportive mother (and a terrific writer herself), who inspired "Critic's Choice" before leaving this world far too soon. Yes, she really did give my previous book a five-star Amazon review.

Acknowledgments

Thank you to the editors of the following publications, where versions of these poems previously appeared:

251: "We'll Always Have Pittsburgh"
The Asses of Parnassus: "The Chair"
The Dirigible Balloon: "The Window"
Light: "Behind Every Cloud," "Critic's Choice," "Funeral for a Friend," "Lives of the Poets," "Love Song," "Parts Unknown," "Progressive Glen" (Several of the Headline Poems were featured as *Light* Poems of the Week)
Lighten Up Online: "The Best Revenge," "Deep in the Sand," "Doing My Part," "Flatteries Not Included," "A Good Long Life," "In the Mail," "Invisible," "The Lilies," "My Life in Music," "No Sale," "Redeeming the Time," "Regrets," "A Show of Hands," "Tennessee," "The Tulgey Wood"
The Orchards Poetry Journal: "Most Likely"
Philosophy Now: "Since You Asked"
The Pierian: "Let Me Live Alone Beside This Lake"
Pulsebeat Poetry Journal: "Martin Scott," "Sailing to Bismarckium"
The Road Not Taken: A Journal of Formal Poetry: "Owed on a Grecian Urn," "The Race Is On," "Thoughts and Prayers"

Contents

Act I: On Writing and Writers

Doing My Part	17
Lives of the Poets	18
The Rime of the Ancient Mariner Summarized	20
I Have Issues	21
Of Making Books	22
Sailing to Bismarckium	23
Owed on a Grecian Urn	24
The Tulgey Wood	26
Hull Hound on My Trail	27
To Arms! To Arms!	28
Deep in the Sand	29
The Write Time	30
No Sale	32

Act II: Lessons Learned

Little Things Mean a Lot	35
Unforgettable	36
The Best Revenge	37
Invisible	38
Regrets	39
A Better World	40
A Show of Hands	41
Flatteries Not Included	42
Redeeming the Time	43
I'm Just Saying	44

Act III: A Sense of Place

Love, Suburban Style	47
Let Me Live Alone Beside This Lake	48
Even the Rain	49
Money Talks (The Universal Language)	50
Tennessee	51
Home at Last	52
Ohi Day	53
We'll Always Have Pittsburgh	54
All Greek to Me	55

Act IV: But Seriously, Folks

The Lilies	59
Martin Scott	60
A Good Long Life (Some Restrictions Apply)	62
Election Day	63
Keeping the Faith	64
Most Likely	66
The Race Is On	67
Just a Minute, Man	68
The Chair	70
Thoughts and Prayers	71
Reflection on the News of a Classmate's Passing	72
Funeral for a Friend	73

Act V: But Wait, There's More!

Love Song	77
The Window	78

Since You Asked	79
In the Mail	80
Betty Spaghetti	81
Double Your Urnings	82
Always Something There to Remind Me	83
Lost	84
My Life in Music	85
Drinking for Two	86
Fancy Cat's Up	87
Progressive Glen	88
A More Perfect Onion	89
Easy Doze It	90
Parts Unknown	91
Here's Mud	92
It's All Relative	93
Spoken Like a True Artist	94
Behind Every Cloud	95
Why the Army Stopped Drafting Poets	96

Writing Out the Day's Events (Headline Poems)

It's a Business Doing Pleasure with You	99
Your Just Desserts	100
I'm Robbin' It	101
Nothing to See Here, Folks	102
Altar Ego	103
It All Happened So Fast!	104
Simply the Best	105
Law for Sale	106
Gone for Gouda	108
The Long Arm of the Law	109
I Think We've Seen This Movie	110

A Few Choice Words	111
Go With the Flow	112
The Last Laugh	113
Great White Hope Not	114
That's the Spirit!	115
We Don't Know Squat	116
Pelf on the Shelf	117
Eel or Faux Eel?	118
A Pitcher's Worth a Thousand Words	119
Driving Miss Crazy	120
Eight O'Glock Bell	121
One More for the Road	122
Sign Me Up!	123
Don't Stop Till You Get Enough	124
What Could Go Wrong?	125
Fishing Lines	126
Bobby, We Hardly Knew Ye (If Only)	127
Anyone's Guess	128
Get a Grip	129
Clocking Out	130
Fool's Gold	131
Loched and Loaded	132
The Windmills of His Mind	133
Full Disclosure	134
Lucky for You, He's Only Mostly Dead	135
Exile on Sesame Street	136
What Are the Odds?	137
Go Figure	138
The Raw Truth	139
Conspicuous Consumption	140
Point of No Return	141
Bobby, Do You Like Movies About Gladiators?	142
Ignorance Is Bliss	143

Barely Profitable	144
What More Can You Ask For?	145
Knot Today!	146
Thank You for Your Patience	147
Identity Prices	148
Owl, I Ask of You	149

Act I: On Writing and Writers

Doing My Part

"A masterpiece from Mr. Kent,
   A classic" (Barnes and Noble)*
But rave reviews don't pay the rent,
   Domestic ones or global.
My book was writ to make you laugh,
   To touch your heart, to thrill ya
With warmth and humor (half and half),
   So *buy* the damn thing, will ya?

*Author's paraphrase. The Barnes and Noble reviewer's exact words were "Please do not contact us again."

Lives of the Poets

Milton (John)
Droned on:
Eden's Gone.
Big yawn.

Wordsworth (Will):
A pill.
So much skill,
But still.

Byron—Gord—
A Lord,
Rarely bored:
He *scored!*

Shelley, P
Sailed free
(Italy)—
Drowned, he.

Browning (Liz),
Bob's Miz;
Hers and his,
Fame is.

William Yeats
Debates
Irish states
With mates.

T.S. El
Did well:
Waste Land hell,
Nobel.

Dr. Seuss
Got loose
On Mateus
And juice.

The Rime of the Ancient Mariner Summarized

Oh Guest, a word:
I shot a bird
Without excuse.
All hell broke loose:
They turned (the crew)
A ghostly hue;
I suffered strife
With Death-In-Life,
Then, rotten luck,
Our ship got stuck.
Was cold, was hot,
But learned a lot.
My torment ceased;
I'm back, at least.
Enjoy—somehow—
The wedding now.

I Have Issues

I buy *The New Yorker,* I read it and then
I rush to my study with paper and pen
To find inspiration has fled once again:
My verse and my fiction fall far short of 10
Except on a scale of, say, 20 or so
(Perhaps more like 5, maybe 4, I don't know).
Ten years I've been writing, with nothing to show;
My dreams of great themes were, it seems, premature.
I pine for a line on a fine sinecure;
Alas, *The New Yorker* is out for damn sure!

Of Making Books

Of making books there is no end,
Or so the ancient scriptures tell;
A lifetime we could surely spend
On just the good ones written well.

But what of those most unsublime,
Unsuited for the test of time?
Great authors will forever be
Outnumbered exponentially,
And scribes with little taste or wit
Can crank out dreck not worth a whit.
The poetaster, romance hack,
The *philosophe,* the science quack,
The TV pundit talking tough,
The quirky local history buff,
The candidate ("I can't be bought"),
The D-list actor we'd forgot,
The prophet with his End Times rap,
The paranoid in tinfoil cap—
Their leaden tomes roll off the press
And soon sell less and less and less
Until at last the bookstore elf
Can toss them on the Closeout shelf,

A waste of paper, time, and ink
Discerning readers may deplore,
And yet, despite what critics think,
Each week we get a hundred more.

Sailing to Bismarckium

(with apologies to W.B. Yeats)

I.

That is no country for old men,
Nor much of one for others.
I would not see the place again,
Not if I had my druthers.

II.

Oh, Grecian goldsmiths wear me out;
They're worse than holy sages.
I find too many now about,
Demanding higher wages.

III.

What's left to do but sound alarms?
Our generation's dying,
While in each other's open arms
The young are ever lying.

IV.

An aged man's a paltry thing,
A tattered coat and so on.
O death, O death, where is thy sting?
It's time to get the show on.

Owed on a Grecian Urn

My name is Keats, I told the clerk,
And I would like to see that vase.
He drew it slowly from the case
And tried to hide a gentle smirk.
"The cost is rather high, young man,"
He said, as though he somehow knew
My purse was empty. This was true,
But then I quickly formed a plan:
I'd lead him to believe (I thought)
That I could lay my hands on more
Than I'd brought with me to the store,
And thus could pay for what I bought.

My credit's good all over town,
I most indignantly replied.
He rolled his eyes, then loudly sighed
And said "Enough; please put it down.
You see, I think I have it sold
Already to a richer chap
Whose bag of silver fills his lap
(He's worth a fortune, I've been told).
So here's the thing—now listen, kid,
You look like the poetic type,
And while you might not buy his hype
Or praise the man for what he did,
To pay my bills is quite a task
And so I take what I can get.
I deal in cash—the safest bet—
And he can pay the price I ask.
One day a world may come in view
Where those with your artistic soul
Have all they need, and full control,
But I can't see that world, can you?"

I left the shop a bitter youth;
It nearly did my faith destroy
Since rich men rarely do enjoy
Such wealth of beauty, wealth of truth.
In later years I'd sadly learn
What happened once I walked away:
Both clerk and buyer died that day,
And no one knows about the urn.

The Tulgey Wood

(Lewis Carrol, Meet Emily Dickinson)

'Twas brillig—yet not time enough
For slithy toves—and yet and yet
Both gyre, and gimble—more than rough—
Within the wabe were falsely met.

And if fair borogrove were all
That mimsy—she of ghostly hue—
Beheld within the sacred hall,
Then rath the momes outgrabe—and do.

The manxome foe with vorpal blade
Was felled—down came it—proudest man,
Of Jabberwock, he, not afraid—
Who heard of—never was again.

Hull Hound on My Trail

Philip Larkin got *around:*
Roué of Hull, a hopeless hound
In spite of looking super-nerdy
(Had to help that he was wordy).
Modern, yet still antiquarian—
Ladies love a louche librarian.

To Arms! To Arms!

I can conquer light verse if you ask,
But when sober I fail at the task,
So do not be alarmed
If you see me well-armed
With decanter, a bottle, and flask.

Deep in the Sand

Read Sartre on a sunny beach?
   I tried it—not a fan.
Nausée, No Exit: out of reach
   For *this* windsurfing man.
A downer, dude, right from the start;
   I don't see his allure. Us
Hippies also hate Descartes,
   But love old Epicurus!

The Write Time

(or, Attention Must Be Paid)

I *have* to write. My tablet's here,
My pencil's sharp, my desk is clear.
Excuses, alibis, distraction
All be gone! Away, inaction,
Far from me; the written word's
My sacred task . . . You hear those birds?
Their tune is lovely . . . I'm digressing.
(Concentrate! Man, stop this messing
'Round, for there's a job to do.)

Now listen, Muse, inspire me; you
And all your sisters, come and visit
In your manner most exquisite.

Muses! Who could think of those?
Athenians, I do suppose—
Say, have you been to Athens lately?
What a city, changing greatly,
Visitors from everywhere . . .

Get back to writing! Hey, you care
To grab a drink or maybe supper?
I could use a pick-me-up, or
Maybe we could see a show . . .

No, *I must write,* so friend, you go
Ahead. I've barely started working;
Let me not be blamed for shirking
My responsibility.

That music: Is it on TV?
There's way too many flutes and saxes.
Really, I should start my taxes
Soon; they will not wait for long . . .

Forget the money; mute the song!
I've *got* to think, to pay attention,
Focus fully . . . Did I mention
I might have to buy a car?
Been looking 'round, both near and far
For just the right one; what a caper . . .

Darn it, where's that sheet of paper?
Ready! Pencil's in my hand . . .

Is dust collecting on the stand
Where books are piled? Just let me clean it,
Then I *have* to write. I mean it.

No Sale

As poet I was pauper so I made a change in style;
I went full-on commercial, then I worked that for a while.
But still I saw no profit and I finally gave up trying.
You can't sell out in poetry—let's face it, no one's buying.

Act II: Lessons Learned

Little Things Mean a Lot

When I was young and green I longed for lots of flashy things:
Some fine guitars, big homes and cars, expensive diamond rings.
Alas, I failed to find the joy such baubles might bequeath,
And now I'd be content if I could simply find my teeth.

Unforgettable

Each night I lie awake and think
On decades worth of errors made:
Those times I failed to make the grade
Or maybe had too much to drink
And said what I should not have said
And did what I should not have done—
I catalog them, one by one,
Although my weary, aching head
Implores me stop and rest awhile.
There's bound to be a heavy cost
For all the sleep I'll soon have lost,
But agonizing's more my style.
Why *did* I purchase for my home
This mattress made of memory foam?

The Best Revenge

I got a girl then lost her, sadly;
  Did my best to love her well.
But though she left me feeling badly,
  Now I'm rich, so what the hell.

Invisible

The young, of course, do not know what I mean:
Invisible's a most unwelcome way
To spend my golden years. I have to say
That life was better back when I was *seen*,

For now I pass through shops and down the street
And spot no ladies looking my direction;
No longer even worthy of inspection,
Wan condescending smiles are all I meet.

Yes, there were those who tried to warn me then:
Son, live each hour of youth like it's your last.
Their voices echo often from the past:
You'll never know such glory days again.

And yet I shall not wear my trousers rolled,
Nor don white flannel down along the beach.
Though young man's clothes today are out of reach,
I bloody well won't dress like someone *old!*

Regrets

In youth I loved Hugh Mannity,
Though love soon seemed a childish trope.
Now he can't measure up to me,
So I'm alone. Signed, Miss Ann Thrope.

A Better World

Everybody makes the world a better place at heart:
Some when they arrive, some others not till they depart.

A Show of Hands

The thumb is there for hitching rides;
Its rules are often useful guides.
The index finger points at things,
The third one wears important rings.
"A promise made," the pinky states,
But Number Two *communicates!*

Flatteries Not Included

To be frank, I'd be further ahead
Had I chosen the words that I said
With more care and precision the way all the *real* strivers do it,
For each fool with a flattering tongue
Soon ascends to a much higher rung
On the ladder of life while I watch from the bottom. Eh, screw it!

Redeeming the Time

My peers have deeper goals where mine are shallow;
They cultivate their lands where mine are fallow
And labor like a band of busy beavers
(Unlike myself, the dean of non-achievers).
Our days are meant for music, revels, dances—
Though some say work won't kill you, why take chances?

I'm Just Saying

That wisdom we're supposed to get from living?
I think mine might have fallen off the truck—
I should have learned by now to be forgiving
And should have learned how not to give a darn.

Act III: A Sense of Place

Love, Suburban Style

Sue spotted him at Starbucks—that was that—
And promptly dumped her brand-new husband Pat.
Within a week she laid him in his grave,
Then afterward at Starbucks fell for Dave,
Who promptly dumped his brand-new wife Renée
And headed south with Sue to 30A.

Let Me Live Alone Beside This Lake

Let me live alone beside this lake
To pass my time in peace and never think
Of money. Give me good red wine to drink,
And only things of beauty will I make.

Let me be awakened by the sun
Each morning as it peeks in through the pines,
And may I, on my canvas or in lines
Composed, redeem the day till evening's done.

Let me in this cottage be complete,
Enraptured by the lark and whippoorwill,
The loon and mourning dove. Let all be still;
No earthly song could ever sound so sweet.

Even the Rain

Even the rain is more beautiful here,
Even the light of the gloam,
Even the music, the food and the beer—
Honey, let's never go home!

Money Talks (The Universal Language)

Just look away, old man; yes, that's my lady.
Strike her from your thoughts, you get my drift?
She can't swayed by flattery or gift,
And frankly you seem more than slightly shady.

Though I might lack your magnate kind of money
(Island mansion, vineyard, massive yacht),
Her needs are very simple, and she's got
Exactly what she wants and more, my honey.

You'll never steal her heart from me. It's true:
Don't hold out hope your riches count for much.
We have our Indiana home; as such,
Who cares that you own three here on Corfu?

No, save your oily European charm
For all the weak-willed tourist women, please.
These beaches and the coastal Grecian breeze
Are nice, but my girl loves it on her farm.

I feared this trip might turn out badly, yet
She begged for time away (to be together).
Now she says it's perfect here; the weather
Warmed us both in ways we won't forget.

Behold, she comes. Don't catch her eye, you hear?
I see that silly smirk across your face;
I'll bet you think I'm easy to replace.
(She smiled in your direction; hmm, that's queer.)

Oh darling, you were joking that I'm dim
This morning; how we laughed! What's that you say?
You've got to make some changes? Here? Today?
Hold on—you're really leaving me for *him?*

Tennessee

I do believe this heat might kill me yet.
Though summer is for some the perfect time,
I would as soon the summer just forget.

The autumn or the spring? A better bet—
Both seasons bless my soul with temperate clime.
I do believe this heat might kill me yet.

Of winters, I have only one regret:
I failed to love them fully in my prime.
I would as soon the summer just forget.

I swear today before the sun has set
I'll perish (not because of any crime)—
I do believe this heat might kill me yet.

The air's insanely hot and soaking wet;
I curse old Mother Nature's paradigm.
I would as soon the summer just forget,

For I am covered head-to-toe in sweat,
Too irritated now to find a rhyme.
I do believe this heat might kill me yet;
I would as soon the summer just forget.

Home at Last

(Song of Naxos)

Could I have dwelt, far back in time and space,
Upon this fertile island in the Sea
And scaled its marble mountains in my youth,
A member of that fabled ancient race
Who taught a brutish world philosophy
To show that truth is beauty, beauty truth?

No spot on earth seemed half as much like home
As when my roving foot first felt the shore
Beneath me. Mystic voices called my name:
Oh Child, returned at last! Now never roam
Again, but find your place forevermore
In this ancestral Eden whence you came.

Ohi Day

The pomp and circumstance are grand
  On Ohi Day, on Ohi Day:
The children march to beat the band
  On Ohi Day this morning.
Their flags the people proudly raise
  On Ohi Day, on Ohi Day
Along the streets and in cafes
  On Ohi Day this morning.

When every leader stands and speaks
  On Ohi Day, on Ohi Day,
He'll swear that *heroes* fight like *Greeks*
  On Ohi Day this morning.
He knows he simply can't go wrong
  On Ohi Day, on Ohi Day
To echo Churchill loud and long
  On Ohi Day this morning.

In years to come, let none forget
  On Ohi Day, on Ohi Day
How much is owed, how great the debt
  On Ohi Day this morning.
May those both young and old recall
  On Ohi Day, on Ohi Day
The reason they turned out at all
  On Ohi Day this morning.

Ohi (OH-hee) Day, 28 October, is one of Greece's most important national holidays. It celebrates President Ioannis Metaxis's 1940 refusal to allow Mussolini to use his country as a staging ground for Italian military campaigns. Upon learning of Metaxis's denial and the subsequent resistance by Greek civilians to Italy's invasion from the north, Churchill observed that "until now we would say that the Greeks fight like heroes. From now on we will say that heroes fight like Greeks." *Ohi* (Όχι) is Greek for "no."

We'll Always Have Pittsburgh

Each day as I'm passing the airport
   I'm struck by a strong urge to fly,
To jump on a plane bound for somewhere:
   Duluth or Des Moines or Dubai.

A travel club called me last summer;
   I wish I had chosen to join.
Who knows, maybe now I'd be seeing
   Dubai or Duluth or Des Moines.

Instead, I'm stuck here on this highway,
   My life going nowhere, in truth,
Still dreaming one day I might visit
   Des Moines or Dubai or Duluth.

All Greek to Me

I loved a Grecian girl whose name was Monica
As well as one I only knew as Dora;
The first I met in port outside Salonica,
The second in the hills of Meteora.

But romance brought me nothing more than static, a
Heart soon badly broken by their cheatin'
(Both Monica and Dora quitted Attica
To sail away with Constantine the Cretan).

It's clear that I might be the biggest dope: Ol' me,
I fall for every lady's "Love me, Stavros!"
No way I'll waste the winter at Ermoupoli—
It's time to try my luck in Epidavros.

Act IV: But Seriously, Folks

The Lilies

The lilies neither toil nor spin,
Yet Solomon would not have been
Arrayed like these, or so we're told:
They live in peace, both young and old,
While humans hustle to and fro
And push and pull and stop and go.

Beware the energetic man,
A slave to his own master plan
To win the race against a rat—
No earthly good can come of that.
Let vain ambition learn to yield
Before these lilies of the field.

Martin Scott

The applause has all ended, the spotlight is down,
    The fans have gone home now to sleep.
I might be the last man awake in this town;
    I've got this arena to sweep.
There are chairs to be folded and bathrooms to clean—
    Some glamorous job, am I right?
But still, it's a living, you know what I mean,
    So I'll be home quite late tonight.

As a young man, I had lots of typical dreams:
    I wanted to be in a band.
But touring the world isn't all that it seems,
    A lesson I'd soon understand
After hearing the actors and singers and such
    Who come here to stand on our stage—
Relationships crumble, and yet in the clutch
    They cling to that show business wage.

I married real early; soon babies arrived.
    We needed security, so
I took this position. Do I feel deprived?
    On balance, I'd have to say no.
My back hurts much more than it did, this is true;
    My hair's getting thinner and grey,
But Sarah and I have a granddaughter, Sue,
    Who comes by to visit each day.

I probably could have gone further in life—
   Perhaps fame and fortune, who knows?
Yet I have had such a good time with my wife,
   And each year the family grows.
Our kids are now married; they all live nearby.
   We see them as much as we can.
We could have been richer, I'm guessing, but why?
   That wasn't a part of our plan.

Hold on—someone else is awake here. It's Jim,
   The lighting guy up in the booth.
(I've recently done a few favors for him;
   He owes me a solid, in truth.)
Hey Jim, there's a flattop outside in the car;
   Could I have a minute or three
To sing an old song and to play my guitar
   While *you* shine the spotlight on *me?*

A Good Long Life (Some Restrictions Apply)

Want to live to 116? The secret to longevity
is less complicated than you think
                                —The Guardian

The headline tells me—boldly, no misgiving—
That I can hang around to 116.
But who on earth could call that life worth living;
I'd lose more than I'd gain, know what I mean?

The ones I dearly love would predecease me,
So very likely I'd be all alone
To beg of death (or doctors) *Please release me;*
I wasn't built to be here on my own.

I'd shuffle to the park, where I'd see no one
To speak with; we'd have nothing to discuss.
New friendship with an old, old man—who'd grow one?
At 116, they'd say "not worth the fuss."

Good entertainment? Gone before my check-out,
And music I might love I'd never find.
Can't live this way, not me; I'll get the heck out
Before I lose my patience or my mind.

The bistros I enjoy will be closed up then,
While new ones I'd be loath to patronize.
So where exactly would I drink and sup then?
(You see what my dilemma here implies.)

Or what if at the pub my favorite Porter
No longer came on draft? What then, my friend?
No, let my time on earth be *sweet* but *shorter,*
And let me leave here happy to the end.

Election Day

They're sweeping up the streets, and none too soon:
These flyers and the posters coming down
Could fill a bin or two. The printers' boon
Creates a massive mess all over town.

Rash promises were made which can't be kept,
For politics is not this way arranged.
The people voted, left, went home and slept,
Believing *this* time things had really changed.

For those who pull the strings, it's purely show;
In shadows is the place true power lies.
That man behind the curtain we don't know
Will always be in charge, and in disguise.

Keeping the Faith

His doctrines were purer than any we'd heard;
   We welcomed him into our movement
And made him a leader to spread the good word,
   To offer our movement improvement.
He chased out the heretics, those on the fence
   Considered not fully committed,
Plus quite a few others (which made little sense),
   Then member 'gainst member he pitted.

But soon came a stranger to challenge our man,
   Declaring him weak in devotion.
He swore he'd provide us a much better plan
   For setting the cause into motion.
We pledged our allegiance and never looked back;
   Alas, we looked not ahead, either—
Another then promised to get us on track,
   So *now* who to choose? Both? Or neither?

New champions began to appear by and by;
   Each promised to be our uniter.
Each threw down the gauntlet and said, "I'm your guy—
   Though others be right, I'll be righter!"
Division begets more division, it seems,
   While wisdom is judged by her actions:
Small quarrels turned ugly, debate sank to screams,
   Old friendships devolved into factions,

And thus it went on, in the way of such stuff:
   Our faith just grew truer and truer.
Since no one's beliefs could be quite true *enough,*
   The faithful were fewer and fewer.
Declaring anathemas ages ago,
   Today we communicate never;
Our ideological purity, though,
   Is currently stronger than ever.

Most Likely

I didn't win Most Likely to Succeed,
    But that's okay;
The guy who did got busted selling weed
    In East L.A.

Best Party Girl was Sherry Vanderloch
    (Oh, *she* was fun).
Not long ago we all had quite a shock:
    She's now a nun.

Most Musical belonged to Brian Bourne;
    He'd play and play.
At 22 he gave away his horn,
    Or so they say.

The Cutest Couple: Beth and Ricky Lotz.
    Things change, of course—
She left him twice, then stuck him with the tots
    In their divorce.

Best-Looking (Male) was easy: Danny Beard,
    My friend with flair.
I saw him just last week, and *that* was weird:
    No teeth, no hair.

Most Popular was Karen Kerns, and how,
    Yet unbeknown
To all (I still cannot believe it now),
    She'd die alone.

I didn't win Most Likely to Succeed,
    And that's okay.
Perhaps I got exactly what I need—
    I'm here today.

The Race Is On

My neighbor found a stick and then I knew just what to do:
I went and picked a pair, so to his one I now had two.
He right away assumed that I might try to take his life,
Which prompted him to drive downtown and get himself a knife.

When I saw his I went to score one with a bigger blade;
He bought another, as did I, and briefly there it stayed.
Next day I made a vow that I would never be outdone,
Then I discovered he had gone and got himself a gun.

What could I do but buy my own (a larger one, for sure)?
This led him to respond in kind with bigger caliber,
And so it went as each of us a greater one would bring
Until I found a rocket launcher—this might be the thing!

Alas, he got grenades. What else? Of course I did the same,
Then I tracked down a shoulder-mounted cannon shooting flame.
Just yesterday I saw him start to make a homemade bomb,
Yet I can build a better one with tricks I learned in 'Nam.

My wife now says I'm crazy and his calls him truly dense.
Some people simply do not get the point of self-defense:
It's not about maintaining law and order (though I try),
It's knowing you have *one more weapon* than the other guy.

Just a Minute, Man

The message reads *Don't Tread On Me,*
Right there for all the world to see
Upon the bumper of his truck
As if to say, "Don't push your luck—
I'm rough, I'm tough, I've got a plan,
A real suburban Minuteman!"
This warning, which he's proud to state,
Is also on his license plate,
His t-shirts (all red, white, and blue),
As well as on his new tattoo.

And yet it always gives me pause,
His pleading revolution's cause,
For never have I heard him say
One word about our HOA
And regulations they espouse—
What color he can paint his house;
Just where to park that truck, and when;
How soon he has to mow again
For grass to be the proper height;
The mailbox brand, the driveway light,
The type of siding, style of fence
His home can have.
                    It makes no sense:
He swears he's free (while I am not),
This "patriot" so quick to spot
A hundred other tyrannies,
Yet strangely silent as to these.
No matter what, he won't rebel
Despite the many ways they tell
Him how he'd better toe the line
In order to avoid a fine.

By now it should be fairly clear
My neighbor's not quite Paul Revere:
He *thought* about enlisting, then
His bone spurs acted up again.
I'm sure he'll take up freedom's fight,
Unless it falls on movie night.
The Tom Paine spirit? Bring that back!
Just keep it off our cul-de-sac.

The Chair

She'd toss her clothes across a chair,
Her stuff was scattered everywhere,
And then one day she wasn't there.

Thoughts and Prayers

My Congressman, surveying last night's carnage
While searching for some way to prove he cares,
Claims I can't pass a law;
The vote would be a draw.
Instead, I offer all my thoughts and prayers.

He says this every time we have a shooting
(And some days killings come our way in pairs):
The problem's not the gun,
So nothing can be done
Except to offer all my thoughts and prayers.

No matter how much blood is shed, his "sorrow"
Is notable for all it never dares:
Archaic strictures, friend,
We never, ever bend,
But I can offer all my thoughts and prayers.

One day perhaps I'll find his house is burning
And see him at a window, trapped upstairs.
I'll shout out from the street,
The circle's now complete—
Here, let me offer all my thoughts and prayers.

Reflection on the News of a Classmate's Passing

Though born into a common time and place,
We companied but little in our youth
Then went our separate ways; we did not try
To stay in touch, nor was there reason why
We should. And yet I felt today, in truth,
The icy air of death upon my face.

Funeral for a Friend

We've got to get together soon,
We say at tragic times like this.
It's been so long, I don't know why.
Hey, call me Monday afternoon!
More idle chat, a goodbye kiss—
How versed we are, both you and I,
In all the same well-meaning lies
We'll tell the next time someone dies.

Act V: But Wait, There's More!

Love Song

(for Jeni)

My darling, please don't ever drive a truck.
You have (in spades) a special kind of pluck,
But no one's quite as prone to getting stuck.
My darling, say you'll never drive a truck.

My darling, please don't ever drive a ship.
It's bound to change the tenor of a trip
If, coming back to port, we wreck the slip.
My darling, swear you'll never drive a ship.

My darling, please don't ever drive a train,
A helicopter, hovercraft, or plane.
Your forte isn't motors in the main—
Now darling, come and drive me wild again!

The Window

(For Grayson)

I opened a window and in came a bird,
   As feathered as feathered could be,
He sat on the sill; oh, he paused at a pillow,
   Then swooped down and landed on me.

The window still open, it let in a mouse,
   As furry as furry could be.
Though not at all worried, she hurried and scurried
   To play with the bird there by me,

When right through the window there entered a cat,
   As hungry as hungry could be.
Pursuing the mouse, he ran all through the house; he
   Then circled and circled 'round me.

Up next through the window: a big shaggy dog,
   As hairy as hairy could be,
Who made a quick beeline for Fred, the fat feline
   Still chasing the mouse around me.

The window invited a passing young deer,
   As agile as agile could be.
Her leap was quite graceful till she got a face full
   Of popcorn knocked over by me.

More fauna arrived in like manner all day,
   As steady as steady could be,
And now I'm supposing I should have been closing
   The window—how silly of me!

Since You Asked

I scorn those callow critics
Who mock my metaphysics,
And offer no apology
For my epistemology.

In the Mail

These mailing lists I find myself upon
Confound me more and more. Did I subscribe
To endtimesprepper, toenailfungusgone,
thethriftybuddha, russianwinesimbibe,
And lonelysingleladies? Did I seek
newpatriotresistanceusa,
tryfreeviagra, membersonlypeek,
Or reikimeditationsdaybyday?

I send these now to Junk—that's not so hard—
Before my Inbox gets completely full.
Goodbye, thesetrickswillsaveonmastercard
And undiscoveredstocktoridethebull.
So long, greatbonustravelpointsabroad,
adealaweekforseniors, iphonehack,
mysugardaddy, fedinsurancefraud,
stopspam—Oh nuts, I need that last one back!

Betty Spaghetti

(A Children's Poem for Adults)

Betty Spaghetti had long stringy hair,
   Just oodles and oodles and oodles.
It hung down her back and it went everywhere
   And looked like a nest full of noodles.

Betty Spaghetti shunned carrots and peas
   As Nettie, her mother, had taught her.
Her father was some kind of really big cheese,
   But got in a lot of hot water.

Betty Spaghetti chose never to wed;
   Who knows what her reticence meant, eh?
However, it's said she was found once in bed
   With gastronome playboy Al Dente.

Betty Spaghetti grew older and cross,
   Refusing to laugh or to smile;
In town many swore she'd been hitting the sauce,
   A red in the Florentine style.

Betty Spaghetti expired yesterday,
   And so my sad tale is all done
Of one *signorina* who's now pasta way
   (I'll close with that terrible pun).

Double Your Urnings

*I bought an urn for $30 to put my dad's ashes in,
but had to remove the original inhabitant first*
—The Guardian

To store Dad's ashes, my concern.
Our thrift shop had the perfect urn;
That lovely vase was secondhand,
But surely Dad would understand.
I laid the thirty dollars down
And took it to my house in town.
Alas, when I removed the top,
I found somebody else's Pop!

Always Something There to Remind Me

Everything reminds me, pet, of you:
This window you once hurled a skillet through,
The gaping hallway hole—you made that, too.
Everything reminds me, pet, of you.

Every day I ache a little more
When I recall the way we were before
You tied me up and left me on the floor.
Every day I ache a little more.

Every time I look I see your face:
In broken glass, each pitcher, plate, and vase,
In shattered heirlooms no one can replace.
Every time I look I see your face.

Everywhere I turn I feel you here;
The bed you burned is one more souvenir.
(Remember? I was sleeping in it, dear.)
Everywhere I turn I feel you here.

Every night I think, my love, of you
And ask myself, "How *did* she misconstrue
Restraining orders right from Judge McCue?"
Every night I think, my love, of you.

Lost

It's fine to have friends and a honey
Provided you're hip to the cost,
Though son, if you run out of money
All is lost.

A girl can sport cute little freckles
And curves to make cold hearts defrost,
But boy, if she spends up your shekels
All is lost.

She'll wiggle and set your heart whirling
Till every good judgment you've tossed.
Alas, when you're short of the sterling,
All is lost.

Good chums avert many disasters
(As long as your signals aren't crossed).
Still, after you're out of piasters
All is lost.

You may be a gay caballero,
The life of the party when sauced,
Yet once you've run dry on dinero
All is lost.

So take my advice if you're willing:
Your treasury, never exhaust!
The moment you haven't a shilling
All is lost.

My Life in Music

Singing server, made good dough
Less than one full year ago;
Record label talks increased;
I got signed, then got released;
Album's in the Closeout bin;
Waiting tables once again.

Drinking for Two

My darling's a dear one; I love her most madly,
   Though friends, I'm downhearted and blue:
She's now on the wagon (alone, rather sadly),
   And here I am drinking for two.

She's hot to have children and won't say how many;
   She'll make a good mother, it's true,
But good times we had, and today don't have any,
   So lately I'm drinking for two.

Our nights on the town tend to end by 8:30;
   For me this is certainly new.
She's prim and she's proper, she's not at all flirty—
   No wonder I'm drinking for two.

The doctor just told us that triplets are coming;
   Big changes expected, a few!
My nerves will be needing a whole lot of numbing;
   I'll have to keep drinking for two.

I spent so much time as a carefree young lad once;
   The debt for those days has come due.
I'll never get back the lean body I had once
   As long as I'm drinking for two.

Fancy Cat's Up

What *does* he think about, my haughty cat,
While staring out his window by the hour?
I do believe he dreams of royal power—
A Caesar on his throne, and more than that.

No doubt he has a picture in his mind
Of maid and servant waiting 'round the court
To serve his needs, to him alone report,
And never fall a single step behind.

How grand are his delusions, and how high
This Lord imagines his proud self to be
Above the scrum of mere humanity,
While we who feed and shelter him stand by.

Progressive Glen

Our suburb's new and squeaky clean,
The whitest place you've ever seen—
The *houses* here, I mean to say,
For color-blindness is our way:
Progressive Glen's one neighborhood
Where folk all talk the talk they should.

We meet each Monday, half-past three,
To hold forth on diversity,
Although (for reasons we don't know)
Caucasians only seem to show.
Minorities live here, you bet;
We've simply never seen one yet.

I'd like to make this very clear:
On poverty, we're quite sincere.
We own life's tough in every way
For those who labor every day.
We *need* cheap housing—that's not hard—
Just not right here in our back yard.

In education, we insist
Upon a comprehensive list:
Humanities—so much to learn!
Plus biz and STEM—so much to earn!
Those charter kids are rightwing tools,
While ours all go to private schools.

Is privilege real? Alas, my friend,
We fear it might not ever end,
So even though we do lament
Our own, we've learned to be content.
Utopia may come; till then,
We'll see you at Progressive Glen.

A More Perfect Onion

I pen this humble ballad
   For a salad.
Oh, pray you not forget us,
   Begged the lettuce;
Don't put it off till later,
   Said the 'mater.

Next time I'll skip the radish
   (Much too faddish);
In future, don't know when'll
   Go for fennel,
But I'll remain a prepper
   Of the pepper.

I nearly cast my ballot
   For the shallot,
Then chose a green medallion
   Called the scallion.
Come Tuesday, Bacchanalia
   Of Vidalia.

Now, cheese: Which one is better,
   Bleu or cheddar?
What's that, a mozzarella?
   Listen, fella:
When you're in *my* gondola,
   Gorgonzola!

Easy Doze It

I'm awake, yet my mind's on a nap.
Getting up in the morning's no longer a snap;
With the dog at my feet and the cat on my lap,
I am free to start planning a nap.

How I love a good late morning snooze,
And the afternoon's also quite nice if I choose.
I have *earned* this reward, I have paid many dues
For my shot at a second/third snooze.

Is it odd, this obsession with sleep?
Oh, I wonder at times if I'm getting in deep—
I've a house that needs cleaning, some clothes in a heap,
And yet here I am dreaming of sleep.

I'll get busy right after I doze.
Yes, I'll sweep all the floors, put away all the clothes;
Heck, I might wash the car, get a haircut, who knows?
Now excuse me, I'm due for a doze.

Parts Unknown

(or, Every Mechanic's Estimate)

Your discombobulator sprang a leak
That rusted out the manitorken springs,
Which cracked the carbomatic where it's weak
And warped the hydropaniformic slings.

This made your floriturbometric struts
Drop down and block the posipinrod flow,
And that stripped out the keratonic nuts;
These hold the transcominions from below.

I think that while the comprostater's out,
Your camterfusion rod should be replaced—
It's disconnected from the spintergout,
So all your pneumocandoms need respaced.

The camaforic fluid's very gray,
Which points to deficlusion in the base.
And though your hemispanic looks okay
I recommend a new one just in case.

Here's Mud

I went out to buy a new bicycle
And found one on sale; now it's mycycle.
Reporter Rick rides on a guycycle,
A who and what, when, where, and whycycle.
James Bond gets around on a spycycle,
The introvert goes for a shycycle,
The Deadhead just wants a good highcycle,
The senator favors a liecycle,
The baker prefers marble ryecycle.

A motor? You won't have to trycycle.
Propeller? That makes it a flycycle.
Circumference? We're now talking picycle.
Sorority? Pi Alpha Chicycle.
Shakespearean curse? 'Tis a fiecycle.
We're even? Let's call it a tiecycle.
A toast? Hey, here's mud in your eyecycle!

It's All Relative

Although my wife's a thousand times the size of any spider,
   She'll scream and run if one should come her way.
And yet I dare not say a word to mock her or deride her—
   She's half *my* size, but scares me every day!

Spoken Like a True Artist

I mean to use the word *chiaroscuro* very soon
  (By noon)
And then to find an offhand way to talk about *trompe l'oeil*—
  Oh, boy!
The world will surely see me as a serious *artiste,*
  At least.

Behind Every Cloud

My car wouldn't start and the bus didn't show;
   The boss blew his top 'cause he could.
No job now, no money, it's 20 below—
   Things aren't good.

The power's cut off, I've got nowhere to turn:
   Old friends all say "broke—sorry, lad"
(Though out on the town they have money to burn).
   This is bad.

No food in my cupboard, the dog ran away,
   Eviction's begun on my flat.
But Sadie just told me she's leaving today,
   So there's that.

Why the Army Stopped Drafting Poets

I'm greatly annoyed, sir,
Each day I'm deployed, sir—
I've little devotion,
Don't want a promotion.
I'm bored more than most here
While standing at post here
And think it a trifle,
This big, silly rifle,
Of which my attention
Has no comprehension.

In discipline lacking,
I *should* be sent packing,
Yet Sam from the get-go
Was clear he won't let go.
Though bad at obeying,
I guess I'll be staying
Since no, I'm not partial
To facing court-martial.
I fail to pass muster?
I'm fine with that, Buster.

Writing Out the Day's Events
(Headline Poems)

It's a Business Doing Pleasure with You

Rupert Murdoch Reportedly Divorced Jerry Hall by Email
                              (Apr 2023)

The subject line *Re: marriage,* then
   The body reads, "Dear Jerry:
Conditions/terms were stated when
   We both agreed to marry.
This union was performance-based,
   Yet came to no fruition,
So now I choose to move in haste
   And phase out your position.

Your contract I shall not renew,
   Effective date next Monday.
We'll skip the exit interview;
   Please clear your desk by Sunday.
I'll gladly recommend you, dear—
   You're pleasant, bright, and pretty—
But first you'll have to sign off here
   (Attorneys, New York City)."

Your Just Desserts

Chefs Team Up for £633 'Four Hands' Banquet in London
(June 2023)

If money doesn't matter
And you'd enjoy a platter
That runs as much as many people's rent,
Then London's now the spot
To show off what you've got
While bragging how your bounty's been well spent.

For those with drive and gumption,
Conspicuous consumption
Is coolly viewed as virtue, not as vice.
Go let the poor eat cake!
Your pleasure's there to take—
You've *earned* it (so you've told us more than twice).

I'm Robbin' It

*Customer Orders Sandwich Before
Trying to Rob Nashville McDonald's*
                (June 2023)

I'll take some fries, a Big Mac, chicken too,
A Coke, I guess, and one more thing from you:
Just crack the drawer and give me all that dough!
(Oh, by the way, this order is to go.)

Nothing to See Here, Folks

Cash-Strapped Taliban Selling Tickets
to Ruins of Buddhas It Blew Up
                     (June 2023)

Our faith demands destructive sacrifices:
Historic sites the heathens find exquisite,
Which now we pray you'll pay to come and visit—
Oh infidel, you won't *believe* these prices!

Altar Ego

US Restaurant Used Fake Priest in
'Shameless' Wage Theft Scheme
(June 2023)

My son, have you been cheating your good bosses?
These noble souls provide so much employment.
Did you get sinful personal enjoyment
Complaining how your wages suffer losses?

Son, walk in simple faith; do not be clever.
A pay stub doesn't merit close attention—
Don't be that wicked servant scriptures mention!
Say ten Hail Marys (or, you know, whatever).

It All Happened So Fast!

Italian Man Cleared of Assault Because Grope
Only Lasted 'Between Five and Ten Seconds'
                              (July 2023)

His lawyer makes no claim of innocence:
"My client's crime was quick. Your honor, hence
He must be cleared; with charges, please dispense."
The D.A. laughs, "Now *that's* a new defense!"

Simply the Best

Amid Pop's Revolutions, Tony Bennett
Was a Steady, Classy Constant
                              (July 2023)

His heart was not in country, rock, or disco,
But standards (oh, and also San Francisco).

Law for Sale

(To the tune of Cole Porter's "Love for Sale")

*Supreme Court Justice Clarence Thomas Took
38 Undisclosed Vacations from Rich Friends*
                              (Aug 2023)

When the only folks I find about
Are rich men with their wallets out,
That's when my bags I pack;
I don't look back.
And I say nothing, heaven knows,
About these trips I don't disclose—
The secret's safe with me,
As all can see.

Law for sale,
Every kind of case law for sale:
Law to give the donor class
Stuff the House won't even pass.
Law for sale.

Who will pay?
Who's my benefactor today?
If you have a pending tort,
Buy a buddy on the Court.
Law for sale.

Let the likes of Harlan Crow underwrite my jaunts;
We're compadres, don't you know—he gets what he wants,
For we share so many cares,
Me and all these billionaires.
New law, old law,
I do what I'm told. Law

for sale.
Enterprising me! Law for sale.
Own a private jet or yacht?
Come and show me what you've got.
Law for sale.

Gone for Gouda

Italian Man Crushed to Death Under Falling Cheese Wheels
(Aug 2023)

Giacomo's warehouse he runs as he pleases;
Now he's no more, for he went to see cheeses.

The Long Arm of the Law

Georgia Sheriff Pleads Guilty to Groping TV Judge
                                                          (Aug 2023)

"A miscommunication, judge, between us—
I merely meant to show her my subpoenas!"
Now Sheriff Coody finally understands
He can't just take the law in his own hands.

I Think We've Seen This Movie

A.I. Brings the Robot Wingman to Aerial Combat
(Aug 2023)

My co-pilot's far too controlling, it's clear
  (Efficient, but not at all brave).
I bark out an order and what do I hear?
  "Afraid I can't do that now, Dave."

A Few Choice Words

*Society of Authors Calls Use of Bad Reviews
for Book Blurbs 'Morally Questionable'*
                    (Sep 2023)

His cover needs a blurb; hey, that's the biz.
I found a short review, such as it is:

*I've never read a book like this before.
The author has no insight, wit, or skill.
He fails to form important thoughts and more;
His "best" work yet is still sophomoric swill.*

Not great, but let me show you how to share
The fulsome praise quite neatly hidden there:

*I've never read a book like this before.
The author has . . . important thoughts and more;
His best work yet.* See boys, that's how it's done—
I dare you now to write a better one!

Go With the Flow

*Family Sues Google After Maps Allegedly
Directed Father Off Collapsed US Bridge*
                              (Sep 2023)

I've never gone this way before,
But Google is the best around—
Say, what's that rushing water sound?
Why can't I open up my door?

Though many friends find Maps appealing,
Now I'm not so sure, you know?
Concern, I think, is apropos
Since I can't shake this sinking feeling.

The Last Laugh

Bob Ross's First TV Painting Goes on Sale for Nearly $10M
(Sep 2023)

In life they sniffed at Ross's work,
Dismissed it with a knowing smirk.
The critics he could not appease,
But now, those happy little fees!

Great White Hope Not

Orcas Sink Fourth Boat Off Iberia, Unnerving Sailors
(Nov 2023)

Call me Ishmael. Sure, okay,
Whatever, dude—just tend the sail.
Captain swears at last today
We're finally gonna catch that whale.
Ahab's not all there, you know,
But me, I never make a fuss.
Ish, man, what's that noise below?
Oh God, the whale is chasing *us!*

That's the Spirit!

*Six-Year-Old Boy Put on Wrong Flight
from Philadelphia to Florida*
                    (Dec 2023)

It's a bad look for Spirit. No-frill
And admittedly cheaper, but still
One grandma got nervous
When customer service
Misplaced her original Will.

We Don't Know Squat

*Florida Couple Famous for Over-the-Top Christmas
Lights Have Been Squatting for 15 Years*
                                          (Dec 2023)

Our neighbors *love* to decorate; at Christmas it's a nuisance,
   Although they're lovely folk, she and her spouse.
December comes: Our neighborhood takes on a new translucence,
   The night sky all aglow above their house.

The day we came to town they were the very first to greet us;
   They helped unload and stick stuff on our shelves.
At first it didn't strike us odd how glad they seemed to meet us
   While telling not one thing about themselves.

It stayed this way for years and years, through every conversation:
   They'd ask about us both and where we'd been,
But offered of their own lives not a scrap of information
   (Nor did they ever once invite us in).

And yet they've been so nice to us as well as to our daughters;
   To tell the truth, we hate to see them go.
It frankly never crossed our minds the Hyatts might be squatters;
   In Florida, though, you never really know.

Pelf on the Shelf

Do You Have 'Bookshelf Wealth'? A TikTok Home
Décor Trend Has Irked Some Bibliophiles
                                        (Jan 2024)

My look is lived-in, always understated:
   A vase, a painting, placed with utmost care.
The books, of course, have all been hand-curated,
   With no pulp fiction titles anywhere.

There's *Huck Finn, Moby Dick* (about a sailor),
   The works of Shakespeare, Steinbeck for my friends,
And also Roth and Updike, Irving, Mailer,
   Plus Zadie Smith to show I'm up on trends.

A paperback looks cheap, in my opinion;
   Collector sets add class here to my shelf,
Projecting airs of scholarly dominion
   (Though I flunked out of English Lit myself).

I choose them by the lovely leather binding;
   I'm keenly conscious of each luscious hue
Which color-matches. I don't need reminding
   That books are there to *read,* you pedant, you!

Eel or Faux Eel?

Reinventing the Eel: First Lab-Grown Eel Meat Revealed
(Jan 2024)

Tofu burger? Sounds low-fat.
Turkey sausage? I'd try that.
Fake crab sushi? Well, hello.
Test-tube eel meat? *No, no, no!*

A Pitcher's Worth a Thousand Words

Sloshed, Plastered and Gazeboed:
Why Britons Have 546 Words for Drunkenness
                              (Feb 2024)

Though soberly some Yanks might mock us,
  Brits maintain a lengthy list
Of terms we coin to honor Bacchus:
  Plastered, papered, pickled, pissed.

Five hundred forty-six exactly—
  Most impressive, don't you think?
To this I say (and not abstractly):
  Mate, let's have another drink!

Driving Miss Crazy

*'You Shouldn't Be Doing That': Female Pro
Golfer Films Mansplainer at Driving Range*
                              (Feb 2024)

My goodness, you're a golfing beast;
You've played for twenty years at least.
What luck! I came to make a change
And found you waiting at the range
With pointers to improve my game.
That said, Sir, if it's all the same
To you, I think I'll swing the way
We do it in the PGA.

Eight O'Glock Bell

Utah Governor Signs Bill Encouraging
Teachers to Carry Guns in Classrooms
(Mar 2024)

Some bullet points on Utah's plan
   That's causing such a flap:
Will Coach McKinley be the man,
Or will our lunchroom lady, Jan,
   Be first to bust a cap?

From here on out librarians—
   So prim and proper, meek,
The Marians, the scary nuns
Equipped and trained to carry guns—
   Won't turn the other cheek.

High caliber of staffers now
   Demands a show of spunk.
The district handbook must allow
A warning shot across the bow
   To say "Feel lucky, punk?"

Some swear this day was bound to come
   And sure enough it did.
When teacher tells you, "Don't act dumb,
Arrive on time, spit out your gum,"
   You'd better listen, kid!

One More for the Road

Belgian Man Whose Body Makes Its Own
Alcohol Cleared of Drunk Driving
                              (Apr 2024)

It's bottoms up, my friends;
This party never ends.
The syndrome that I've got
Means I can do a "shot"
At home, at work, a club—
The world is one big pub!

They tell me not to drive
So I can stay alive:
I'm crocked around the clock
Sans bourbon, gin, or bock.
My outlook, I would say,
Is glass-half-full each day.

Sign Me Up!

*Michigan Woman Found Living Inside Rooftop
Store Sign with Desk and Coffee Maker*
                                 (May 2024)

This apartment ain't much, but it's mine:
Got my laptop and one power line
For a small coffee maker
And printer. "I'll take 'er,"
I said, "I have *prayed* for a sign!"

Don't Stop Till You Get Enough

*Michael Jackson Was More than $500M
in Debt When He Died in 2009*
                              (June 2024)

Bubbles' friend, trouble's friend:
MJ, late King of Pop,
Earned a celebrity
Nobody had

Dancing and singing so
Cynosuristically.
Managing money, though?
Michael was *Bad*.

What Could Go Wrong?

Elon Musk Says Neuralink Will Test Brain
Implant on Second Patient in Next Week or So
(July 2024)

"This rich man said he'd pay to chip my brain."
(His vibe is Dr. Evil, in the main.)
"I can't see cause for worry here, can you?"
(It's not so hard to think of one or two.)
"I'll be a pioneer—that's kinda groovy!"
(Dude, have you never *seen* a sci-fi movie?)

Fishing Lines

Wild Sharks off Brazil Coast Test Positive for Cocaine
                              (July 2024)

Now even sharks will act, from this day hence,
With narcissistic overconfidence.
We'll know them by their edgy manic grins
And little silver spoons around their fins.

Bobby, We Hardly Knew Ye (If Only)

Street Food: RFK Jr Boasts of 'a Freezer Full of Roadkill'
(Aug 2024)

If Bobby hasn't wormed his way
   Inside your brain to date,
He's trying harder every day
   (Though still not doing great).

That food now in his freezer's not
   The kind most want to eat.
What's next? He owns a camel lot
   And sells exotic meat?

His fauna tales are deeply odd,
   The ones he dares to share—
You *know* there's more, and worse, by God,
   But those we couldn't bear.

Anyone's Guess

Speculation Rife About Banksy's
London Murals After Five Appear
            (Aug 2024)

One week brings five new works, and that's terrific—
How rare that Banksy's ever so prolific.
This enigmatic artist makes a splash
With each reveal (though clearly not for cash).

We never seem to see him, some have written,
Yet cameras cover every inch of Britain.
It's cool these little critters made the scene,
But who the hell can tell us what they mean?

Hold on, his rep now squelches speculation.
Well, that's a shock—the right interpretation
Demands we *shun* interpretation. Yup,
He merely put them here to cheer us up!

Get a Grip

Players Using Toy Claw Game Surprised by
Live Groundhog Among Stuffed Animals
(Aug 2024)

My cousin, Punxsutawney Phil, each year will make the news,
  The biggest headline whore you ever saw,
And yet, between the two of us, who's really paid some dues?
  A *shadow*? Buddy, please—I faced the *claw!*

Clocking Out

Wells Fargo Worker Found Dead at
Her Desk Four Days After Clocking In
                      (29 Aug 2024)

I long for more employees like Denise,
Who slaves away—I've never seen her skive.
Observe her mien, that look of perfect peace,
Remaining at her desk till way past five.
Promotion's all but certain, I can tell.
Oh, by the way, what *is* that awful smell?

Fool's Gold

Sixty Is the New Golden Age:
Meet the Stellar Generation Hitting This Milestone
                                        (Sep 2024)

Some writer claims I'm in my prime,
   Which I deem damn insensible.
He swears I've hit life's perfect time—
   I say that's indefensible.

My knees now hurt, both hips, my back;
   To women I'm invisible.
My daily mood is mostly black
   And rarely am I risible.

My sagging abs reveal I'm old;
   Can't find a way to flatten 'em.
If sixty is the age of gold,
   Don't let me live to platinum.

Loched and Loaded

At a Remote Scottish Pub, a Pint Worth Hiking 20 Miles
(Sep 2024)

Across the Scotch Highlands did old Angus roam
   In search of a pint or some whiskey.
Last call, and now all should be heading for home:
   "I think I'll stay here, lads—too risky.
My trek is a long one, and I'm a pit bissed
   (I mean *a bit pissed*—I've drunk plenty).
This evening's been one that I wouldn't have missed;
   I could stumble one mile, but not twenty!"

The Windmills of His Mind

Boris Johnson: We Considered 'Aquatic Raid'
on Netherlands to Seize Covid Vaccine
                              (Sep 2024)

A plot was planned at Number 10
By BoJo and his Merry Men
To cross the Channel late at night
And steal vaccine shots—crazy, right?
In retrospect, one has to laugh:
It's not his worst idea by half.

Full Disclosure

*Oregon Police Find Bag Full of Drugs Marked
'Definitely Not a Bag Full of Drugs'*
                              (Oct 2024)

Their bag was clearly marked to fool the cops
In case of any routine traffic stops.
The officer they got misread the "not"
And right there on the spot things went to pot.

Lucky for You, He's Only Mostly Dead

Kentucky Man Declared Brain-Dead
Wakes Up During Organ Harvesting
                       (Oct 2024)

On balance he got lucky,
This patient from Kentucky.
The doctors were mistaken;
His time came to awaken.
He sprang up with a shiver:
Let go—hey, that's my liver!
I gave my heart to Jesus,
And He wants all the pieces!
I'm down for a donation,
But not till expiration!

Exile on Sesame Street

Children's Authors Frustrated by
Rise in Celebrity-Penned Titles
                    (Oct 2024)

Keith Richards wrote a children's book?
   That market needs some narrowin'.
His editors took one good look
   And laughed, "We spell it *heroine*."

What Are the Odds?

Universe Would Die Before Monkey with
Keyboard Writes Shakespeare, Study Finds
(Nov 2024)

A million chimps can type until the world has ceased to be
And never pen a Hamlet, Ceasar, Lear, or Richard Three.
Surprised? I must confess, my friends, I lost the urge to bet
On random writing monkeys once I saw the internet.

Go Figure

*Macy's Says Single Employee Was Responsible
for Hiding up to $154M in Expenses*
         (Nov 2024)

Accountants in green eyeshades keep the books;
From time to time there's numbers they might miss, guy.
A dollar here or there? Nobody looks,
But Macy's, man, things don't add up with *this* guy!

The Raw Truth

The Truth About Raw Milk and Why Experts
Are 'Absolutely Horrified' by the Trend
        (Nov 2024)

You fear no flu, no bad bacteria,
Salmonella or diphtheria.
Mind and body, you're a prize,
But love, I can't look pasteurize.

Conspicuous Consumption

Crypto Entrepreneur Eats Banana Art He Bought for $6.2M
(Nov 2024)

Credible, edible,
Parthenocarpical
Fruit sells for millions (it's
Bought à la carte).

Justin, the buyer, then
Quite ostentatiously
Tries to prove taste by
Consuming great art.

Point of No Return

'Mummy Would Prefer You Not to Do That':
How 'No' Became a Dirty Word in Parenting
(Dec 2024)

Now, don't say Mummy isn't fun,
But darling, some things just aren't done.
It's better, dear, if we should choose
To *not* steal Conor's coat and shoes,
And won't it be so jolly if
We *don't* shove Carly off a cliff?
Why, yes, you'd be within your rights
To punch out little Liam's lights
And leave him with a head that's reeling—
Honey, that's a valid feeling,
Rooted in your own sweet psyche.
(How'd I raise this monster? Crikey!)
Still, I think we'd be ahead
To go for tea and cakes instead.

Bobby, Do You Like Movies About Gladiators?

To Show His Health Credentials, Kennedy Ditches His Shirt
(Dec 2024)

Bobby, Bobby, he's our man,
Buffest of his Bay State clan!
Rarely do our Cabinet Secs
Boast a set of sculpted pecs.

Fears no virus, dreads no germ,
Brain half-eaten by a worm—
Sadly (should we cry or laugh?)
Bob was left the lesser half.

Ignorance Is Bliss

Feeling at Home? New App Lets US
Homebuyers See Neighbors' Politics
(Dec 2024)

The couple to our left is to our Right,
And now we barely sleep a wink at night.
We wonder: Are they equally bereft
To learn we're on their right but on their Left?

Barely Profitable

*A Silicon Valley Nudist Resort Is on Sale for $30M,
But Will Its New Owner 'Go Textile?'*
                              (Dec 2024)

This camp's for sale, but nudist, be alert:
The buyer's trying *not* to lose his shirt.
One business rule will always stay the same:
You've got to have some skin, boy, in the game.

What More Can You Ask For?

*Volkswagen Van That Survived Palisades Fire
in Los Angeles Is a 'Beacon of Hope'*
 (Jan 2025)

The hippies knew
A thing or two:
VW vans
Are maybe man's
Best motor deal.
So much appeal:
No speed, no tricks,
But cheap to fix;
No muss, no fuss,
This microbus,
And now we learn
The thing won't burn!

Knot Today!

Joy as Thailand's Same-Sex Couples Can Marry at Last
                                    (Jan 2025)

Unbridled joys
Bring tears, a lot:
Two girls or boys
Now Thai the knot.

Thank You for Your Patience

I Heard Back About a Job Application 48 Years Later
                              (Jan 2025)

Dear Applicant, it seems your file
   Was wrongly set apart
And stuck inside a drawer awhile.
   So, how soon can you start?

Identity Prices

Man Pleads Guilty to Making and
Selling More than 30,000 Fake IDs
(Feb 2025)

His work? Bar none,
   The best I've seen—
Wish *I'd* had one
   At seventeen!

Owl, I Ask of You

Canadians Get Chance to Feed Rodents
Named After Old Flames to Owls
                    (Feb 2025)

I'd like to think I'm too mature concerning my ex, Pat,
  To wish her harm now (never mind the rumor),
Yet gladly I bestowed her name upon a hapless rat
  And paid to watch a spotted owl consume her.

I swore the wound Pat left had healed, though clearly that's not so.
  The if and buts, the wherefores and the whethers
All leave me second-guessing, but today at least I know
  Hope really, truly *is* the thing with feathers.

About the Author

Steven Kent is the poetic alter ego of writer and musician Kent Burnside. A Pushcart Prize and Best of the Net nominee, he is published in *251, Asses of Parnassus, The Dirigible Balloon, The Hypertexts, Light Poetry Magazine, Lighten Up Online, New Verse News, The Orchards Poetry Journal, Philosophy Now, The Pierian, Pulsebeat Poetry Journal, The Road Not Taken: A Journal of Formal Poetry, Snakeskin,* and *Well Read.* He has authored more than 800 permanent entries in the *Omnificent English Dictionary in Limerick Form.* Steven's collection *I Tried (And Other Poems, Too)* was published in 2023 by Kelsay Books.

His website is:
kentburnside.com

www.ingramcontent.com/pod-product-compliance
Lightning Source LLC
Chambersburg PA
CBHW022012160426
43197CB00007B/402